NECTAR AND SMALL

poems by

Jacqueline Balderrama

Finishing Line Press
Georgetown, Kentucky

NECTAR AND SMALL

Copyright © 2019 by Jacqueline Balderrama
ISBN 978-1-64662-090-6 First Edition
All rights reserved under International and Pan-American Copyright Conventions. No part of this book may be reproduced in any manner whatsoever without written permission from the publisher, except in the case of brief quotations embodied in critical articles and reviews.

ACKNOWLEDGMENTS

Grateful acknowledgement is made to the editors of the following journals in which these poems or versions of these poems appeared, sometimes under different titles:

Anomaly: "The Flood I"
Canary: A Literary Journal of the Environmental: "Without the Flood"
Halophyte Zine: "Neighborhood as Labyrinth"
Swamp Ape Review: "Speculation on Disappearance" and "The Flood III"

Grateful acknowledgement is also made to the Taft-Nicholson Environmental Humanities Center and their wonderful staff for their accommodations, shared knowledge, and inspiration in Centennial Valley, Montana. Thank you especially to the Dee Foundation and the University of Utah English Department for funding this Exaltation in the Valley residency during a week in the summer of 2017. I offer a heartfelt thanks to the residency cohort for your attentiveness, friendship, and guidance. The bulk of these poems were first drafted during this experience.

Publisher: Leah Maines
Editor: Christen Kincaid
Cover Art: Jacqueline Balderrama
Author Photo: Jesus Huerta Jr.
Cover Design: Elizabeth Maines McCleavy

Printed in the USA on acid-free paper.
Order online: www.finishinglinepress.com
also available on amazon.com

Author inquiries and mail orders:
Finishing Line Press
P. O. Box 1626
Georgetown, Kentucky 40324
U. S. A.

Table of Contents

Without the Flood 1
American Goldfinch / *Spinus tristis* 2
Abandonment 3
Dwellings and Decay 4
American Kestrel / *Falco sparverius* 5
From the Lookout 6
Tracing the Storm from Girlhood 7
Western Grebe / *Aechmophorus occidentalis* 9
Postcard of the Watershed from Jordanelle Reservoir, UT 10
Rufous Hummingbird / *Selasphorus rufus* 11
The Flood I 12
Short-eared Owl / *Asio flammeus* 13
Speculation on Disappearance 14
Outside 15
Swainson's Hawk / *Buteo swainsoni* 16
The Flood II 17
Red Butte Creek at Bonneville Glen 18
American Avocet / *Recurvirostra americana* 19
Poem with Attempts to Reduce Waste Or Warding Off the
    End of the World 20
Tomorrow 21
Sandhill Crane / *Antigone canadensis* 23
The Flood III 24
Mapping 25
Red-naped Sapsucker / *Sphyrapicus nuchalis* 27
This Side of the Escarpment 28
Tree Swallow / *Tachycineta bicolor* 29
Neighborhood as Labyrinth 30
Notes 31

for my sisters:

Elizabeth, Katherine, Mary

Without the Flood

There's not just one story of disappearance
in a one-hundred-year-flood zone, where runoff
from the Santa Ana had all my life been dry or nearly,
which is to say the flood is never coming.
My sisters and I lived near alley-like fields marked by the negative
space of fenced-in backyards, their overhanging fruit:
crab apples to be cut down in five years
apricots, pomegranates. We named a dog there
and pet it through the chain-link
a few fingers at a time until we were told,
Top Paw was taken to the pound.
Far off, the missing river partly cemented
heats itself. Can a flood happen without water?
In the field, we threw clods of dirt into overgrown corrals
of jimson weed, its trumpet blooms, and abandoned horse sheds.
What belonged to the river was nothing.

American Goldfinch / *Spinus tristis*

During the retreat in Centennial Valley, the first bird spots
his perch on a tall stalk of grass I glimpse from the car window.
He sits in his summer colors—brilliant yellow
with black and white tipped wings, tail, and cap,
among thistles and shrubs leading to aspen leading to Douglas fir
leading up the side of the mountain.

Come fall, in brown feathers, he might be lost
in landscapes of hushed greens or snow.
Now a spot found like the spouting breach of a whale
across the multitude of waves.

Abandonment

Up the forest hillside, we carry ourselves into the thicket.
Dense and narrow, some living trees stunt one another with shade.

Indian paint brush, clusters of white yarrow, yellow cinquefoil,
we must be reintroduced to wild strawberry disguised without fruit.

My mother used to ask after nighttime prayers, *what was your happy
 thing today?*
But I've learned there are limitations in only acknowledging the good.

Into the valley, a bear travels for miles toward the carcass of a cow
poisoned by larkspur. I found strawberries, the first one, so bitter.

Why should we think that only the gold ring thrown into the ocean
in the story should come back to us in a fish?

Whatever else we've abandoned in hopes of anonymity can and will
return in the air, the water, the baked earth, our bodies.

What was your happy thing? I will ask my husband before sleep,
when I am home again. *What was your sad thing today?*

Dwellings and Decay

We carried colors
of our beach visits and not
just the yellow pail
Dad said was headed to China
fifteen years ago.

We carried colors of inland summer picnics, water-balloon fights, takeout suppers and let the rivers carry them too. Lipstick-ringed bottles, polymer bags, bubble wrap, lighters, bottle caps, toothbrushes, old sandals, fishing tackle

                    : the dwellers of negative space
                    buried, sunk, scattered : dwelling on us

where young albatrosses decay from
damp feather to hollow bone to bill.
The wind performs gradual autopsies.
Their wings a spun frame,
their wings woven lines,
not wings.

          And the mass at their centers is, and it is, and it is.

American Kestrel / *Falco sparverius*

The kestrel has eyes in the back of its head,
markings of another face, the way Janus
looks back into the old year and forward into the new.
We've painted similar masks less for naughty children
and more for what follows accumulating slowly
behind us.

When it catches up, we think we can organize thoughtlessly
like ants or bees or the birds in *The Birds*.
But truthfully, we count on dying by then,
that it doesn't really matter. Without us,
the tree that falls in a forest doesn't make a sound
doesn't even fall.

Unlike the kestrel who, against the wind, flies in place,
we move so the world blurs around us.

From the Lookout

Forgiving ourselves routinely is the overgrowth
that fire failed in our prevention. We must stumble over this
on each self-inspection. My kindling is a growing shadow
of snags and fallen trees weakening the bend of the living
when saplings must be tested by the wind.
Gone the small sacrificial fires, gone the gathering of brush.
So when it happens, we may alight and never be extinguished.

There are new ways of doing for all of us
who want to have, want have been enough.
Where has the creek gone—grown over by green?
I listen to its soft rush over stones,
follow the path that follows the stream to the clearing
where bluebird and swallow catch insects midflight.
Thunder sounds, echoing off the mountains.

Tracing the Storm from Girlhood

Over my shoulder,
the dried grasses, oak trees,
bright sky world from which I entered
the storm drain
became an O of light
diminishing to a point
the farther I went
flashlight in hand
toddling my feet on either side
of the small, steady stream
expecting the tunnel to cut
into complete absence
at some other point
where leaves or carwash suds or rain
coursed the underworld of pipes,
its many mouths
swallowing stray kittens,
escaped pet snakes,
and local raccoons who popped in
now and again from curb drains—
these the expected occupants
in the network that promised
to lead to some inescapable blue
stitched with light and rising,
but this was inland enough
to not lead me to the ocean.

I lived among the remnants
hearing two beats of a drum
over my head. What was I beneath—
some road, some great pulse of landscape?
And when only the flashlight
was the source of light, and I turned
this way and that, the tunnel was less

a beginning and end, less a direction
of water trickling one way
through the hollow.
Moss grew in its seams,
grew in-between my fingers,
water murmuring of all it traced
that day and over centuries
spilling through bodies, around stones,
thinning earth.
Whether I'd turned back or gone
straight through with the dying
of the flashlight
and rising of the moon,
I know I am still within:
darkness, the dim
outlines of trees.
I draw with water
again and again,
the scrawling stick
measuring rainfall.

Western Grebe / *Aechmophorus occidentalis*

Among swans and ducks on the far side
of Upper Lake, two red-eyed grebe
pace with their reflections—
four birds—two above, two below
in a blurry underworld. During mating season,
these two above might mimic neck bends and preening
before rushing the water, standing upright on their far back feet
with extended necks while the reflections below dive in unison
into the deeper waters of winter on the sheltered coast.

Postcard of the Watershed from Jordanelle Reservoir, UT

You and I perform the ritual of touching water—
cold and tame from the snowmelt—
but cannot help envisioning better-known lakes
and seeing their missing dark pines.
Here, the few trees are bare and low before the rocky beach
shushing...wave for small wave
over stones and descending, flat, skipped rocks—rose, tan, white.
In the rippled, black driftwood, a hollow eye
shares the insect view of the stonescape.
Above, no birds, save one flying off against the red and gray horizon
of eyelids closed. Now is when pieces of me are borderless—
whale fall carcass for crabs, hagfish, osedax worms,
in a deep unrest upon the ocean floor.
Then, you speak, pointing to the embankment,
a line ending the reservoir, dividing our view
from snowcapped mountains we thought we'd reached.
Drain the lake of its stars, and the valley towns beneath,
flooded decades ago, might shake off their shadow.
And this should be no surprise. We drive home,
down to the dried floodplain, to where they've built the city.

Rufous Hummingbird / *Selasphorus rufus*

Flashes of red and copper, then
green and brown females for breakfast at the feeder.
Will I see this one again, migrating from Canada
to Southern Mexico, a blip across the highway
as we drive in our cars?

The nest found in foliage yesterday beside the aspens
might be refurbished in later years, the female
gathering moss and webs for repair.
She will feed her two chicks
akin to John the Baptist's diet:
nectar and small, crushed insects.

The Flood I

but i had no appetite / not after weeks of this / filling and too few vessels / gray in as many tones as an old film / the storm had puddled all color into one dark sea / revived memory or premonition / which is to say / and so goodbye to the mud houses dissolved / goodbye to the unlucky newspapers / and had we left our old selves out there too / in the current to some void / blank faced and tired / like all our givings-up / current versions would have to suffice / i tell myself / i'd prefer to imagine first signs of life / green / green / green / from the winter water burial / or our ancestor creatures driven to the water's edge / to march the shore / or to draw lines in the sand with their heavy tails / but starting fresh is starting nowhere

Short-eared Owl / *Asio flammeus*

A misty figure stands on the road to Lower Lake
as in a film noir just before the voice-over,
a guide who might take one or a select few
through the triad of water, earth, sky. In the silence,
it faces us, or not. The cows, whose pen this is,
have moved to the far edges. The road, which moves
through the pen, bare except for this one.

Then at the sound of the car door, it spreads and lifts off,
a mass of wing in gray, brown, and cream silently gripping the air.
It flies low, landing after several yards, out of sight,
far enough to be gone.

Speculation on Disappearance

My mother tells me last night, she discovered a door
in the house to a room where her father
was feeding deer from the car window in Yosemite,

> because everybody used to play
> host in the forest saying, *I am saving you
> for me. I am saving you.*

Let the gift disappear like a magic trick,
the refuse that's brought be forgotten
remains, nesting against fence or roots.

> That is the sleight of the indestructible.
> Bury the waste. Bury the seed. Bury the body.
> Something will emerge from the soil.

Outside

I drive out of town and still farther
toward industrial storage buildings, the marsh,
dry hills and fenced-in space marked as a nursery.
But it is winter. There are no plants. I pass
road kill, the stench of skunk and arrive
at the dump, all because my place has no green bin
and I have followed the instructions of the woman
at the scales with my one bag of compost.
But she must have misunderstood the veggie tops
and peels kept frozen for months, because
on all sides, trucks are being unloaded of brush,
old carpet, broken furniture into a moderate deep.
Something might sort through it. I tell myself,
I have come too far not to empty the bag.
It is gone and not gone.
I search higher ground for the burial site of it all.
A tractor moves over uneven terrain
scattering a mass of birds. They fly up like lead
against a cloudy sky, circle, and return. Perhaps this is the spot,
magnets spinning one over the other.
Attraction, repulsion, come, go, come.

Swainson's Hawk / *Buteo swainsoni*

At first, dark against the slab of sky
any bird without a name. Then,
over a layer of dew, the advancing light
settles dawn's inky shades
into a monochrome gradually colored.
And now the bird—
light morph, red bib—turns in profile
like Horus, the distant one.

Most photos display the raptor perched
on a fencepost like the bust
of some momentary patron.
The placard—Buteo swainsoni—
is a murky pool. In reflection:
Swainson, an English naturalist and artist of 1827
sits with his specimen for preliminary sketches.
But this bird, one side of a thaumatrope,
is captured and escaping.

Swainson mistakes it as one overseas
thinks he glimpses his neighbor
in the grasslands in which he thought
himself alone. From retrospect
others determine it is not a common buzzard but a new face:
two Swainsons and the lithograph between them
a window.

Pressed from this origin, Swainson's hawks
one by one, pull off, circulate before winter
in the company of turkey vultures and Mississippi kites,
their shallow V wingspans, distant waves
in a kettle of thousands churning on toward South America.

Still midsummer here, this Swainson's hawk alone
with the morning and its observers.
From the nest of my eye, its breast feathers catch
the wind, and it embraces the absence, flying
toward me and then past and then away.

The Flood II

with the flood was the inclusion of all we'd seen / glancing off our lives / onto the blank page of our imaginings / so that green was red / and the patterned disks spinning / my childhood too / had found a way to spiral back to the front / it was easier to think of being chased / into a bird then / that our animal fear would / offer escape / can you picture it yet / the body folded into a fraction of its size / but the bones in the forelimbs still mapping / a common path / in this metamorphosis i try not to forget / meanwhile there is a place where i am watching homing pigeons / on their 3pm flight of figure-eights above my friend's childhood house / while on the telephone wires / a hawk has learned the hour too / my head's bent back till they finally land / on the neighbor's roof and return to their coop for feed / she tells me her father will pet them / but they do not have names

Red Butte Creek at Bonneville Glen

She has been holding her breath
for miles, breaching only in half-hidden spurts
of flora and fauna like this. Today I've found
a bird refuge and creek segment—
an inhale of color and breeze and chimed sounds
before she's all swallowed again.
O interlude to a mute march downstream.
        O tapped vein descending from the heart.
                O green dash on a map of stone.

Once it felt as if the rivers in this city
were all cemented over and channeled through pipes.
Now, framed by the backyards of nearby homes,
this creek emerges nymph-like
in her magnetism of light and waving branches.
She holds the secret of June sucker and crayfish
on the undersides of resting stones.

This is what my mother-in-law promises
another day on her visit. But I don't believe it
until a crayfish appears in our path, dead,
found before by someone else or by their dog
(too exact and immediate for a prank),
and later on the same walk I see two fish
in the shadows near the pipe's mouth.
Before, I wanted to say the creek fills
with notes traveling beneath the city
until her song pours out this glen.
But mostly I'm thinking of lunch now,
of my mother-in-law, years ago
scavenging the stones
in the creek she remembers,
holding crayfish over the fire.

American Avocet / *Recurvirostra americana*

The silhouettes of five knee-deep in water
dip their upturned beaks into the shallow pond.
We might imagine the avocet this way every morning,
faded with mist or their mating colors
of blush and black in perfect view with us
disappeared and not sidestepping the cowpats
strewn about the bank.

The females may
lay eggs in the nests of other birds,
raise the chicks that hatch
in their own, incubate fake nests as decoys.

What to say for a bird whose place is displacement?
The clutch of eggs beneath the hem
of feathers is yours and mine.
If we cannot run or fly fast enough
to chase predators from our nests,
at least our voices will rise,
arrive first, then pull us closer.

**Poem with Attempts to Reduce Waste Or
Preparing for the End of the World**

Like some, I have modeled my home as microcosm
for a desired future: cleaning with lemon halves,
boxed baking soda, vinegar, remembering
canvas bags and saving twist ties
as if one day there really won't be anymore.
My husband and I talk ourselves into buying
just a little meat wrapped in brown paper.
We let the fruit roll about in the cart.
We brush with bamboo toothbrushes,
line the trash bins with newspaper.
And yes. And good. But still,
you danced to the car and shattered
the milk jug before either of us could be reimbursed.
I've kept the light on all day
for two succulents that probably won't make it.
When we let ourselves out,
occasional plastic straws or cutlery sneak by
at the bottom of the to-go bag.
We planted the vegetables too late in the summer.
We grimaced at the saltiness of homemade toothpaste.
We went searching for an outlet box on the side
of the house for a light over the kitchen door
and scared a bird right out of its home
in late winter, the middle of the night.

Tomorrow

Framed visions of grasslands and mountains replace the windows. Surrounding me: approaching trains, buffalo dipping and raising their beards from swirling reflection. Beneath a clear, hot sky, two cowboys in blue, dusted pants break a chestnut pony when elsewhere on a small canvas, a figure in feathered headdress sits on a footstool, inspecting the painted painting of a similar self— but one who carries a spear on the back of a rearing horse. What attraction is this? Is mine? I admire sunsets or sunrises. There is no rest until I complete the improvised loop and return my map. Yet, this old world of tomorrow churns still...

    I take the cement path to the 17 Bus.

Light has dimmed,   tucked itself into buildings,

streetlights.

As I drift,   pigments sink further   into a glass of thinner,

piling the mountains gray and uneven   between the slats

    of city blocks.

Each morning, it all might be reversed into   yellow,

magenta,   and ultramarine.

Each morning, the narrow   beams of light above

                    the paintings

I trust will turn on   and make all the difference.

            So far   there have been new days.

Tonight,   in the question of it   —Darkness. We

lie in wait,   clocks counting quietly beside us.

Sandhill Crane / *Antigone canadensis*

Two perhaps mates stand in the tall grass
of the wetland, gray on gray in another morning's light,
disappearing as they bow to damp ground
for grains and larval insects.
Their heads reappear capped red in scattered beams.
Though vagrants of East Asia, I recognize this spot
from a painted fan purchased in Beijing—
two red-crowned cranes in a huangshan pine.
What survives in these relatives
that they are estimated to have lived 10 million years
in grasslands and marshlands like this?
Will we ever be allowed this kind of being?

The Flood III

we baptized / sang to / and enclosed our animals / we dropped our dresses into the stagnant / salt water / on fishing line / to crystalize / we straightened our curls in the bath / we wished for large breasts and pale skin / we pretended to faint / in our dreams when we had been found / under the bed / we eclipsed the light contorting our bodies into the monster / we learned to never open / the creaking door or listen / too long to the murmuring vents / we were the conscience of the reflection / small song bird to the giantess on screen / saying / yes / no / wait / we were immortal for a time / isn't everyone / starting each day with play / rewinding the bad / we learned to hold our breath / learned that someone always dies in the water tunnel / they could not be born again / we suspected / certain faces / parrot spoke the phrases / that'll be the day / kiss me / watch out / we were always right about being afraid / of the dark / we scarified our hearts to sixteen-years-old / we told our eyes what they should emit / we married the pairs of animals / we buried tiger eye and amethyst beneath the deck / forgot / and drew spiral maps / we montaged the chores and outfits / too exhausted for decision / among the lookalike waves / we asked where am i / exchanged land for la la la / and crept into the haul / there would be no receding / of the waters / tonight

Mapping

Upon my revival, I find I have long, thick hair.
Some are convinced it is a wig,
but I tell them to pull,
and they hold on as I walk away.
I'm still walking.
I pull out green lovebirds nesting
in one of the braids. They chew my fingers,
and I throw them into the air.
My hair has started tenting trees.
I find leaves, feathers, lost paper planes.
From water I emerge fully covered.
My hair has caught fish again,
fish that tug on the split ends.
When I've drawn my hair out,
it dries like a sail over the blue
haze when there's wind
enough. The strands expand
a network of threads
joining my body to the hair
to the trees, to the chapel,
to the museum in which we see our ancestor,
a cave woman enclosed in a diorama,
demonstrate the use of a stone.
Before, when my hair was mine
—still brown but thinner and smaller—
I could run my hands through it,
I could heat it into shapes. Is hair how
we recognize the back of ourselves?
I sit with two mirrors.
This hair is too much
for one representation.
What shall I ask it?

I've traversed the streets,
but the birds return.
I am my self in the hair,
my self a point
when the hair is so many
places at once,
my hair that sheds like spider web
or tickles the inside of my arm
that draws labyrinths
that has taken new names
for itself: ivy, smoke, pendulum.
I try to think I am its center,
but it's grown so I am unseen.
Will it engulf me in a cocoon?
Will it suspend me in a tree?
It is only a matter of time.

Red-naped Sapsucker / *Sphyrapicus nuchalis*

There, there, I am told, a sapsucker
perches to the right, mid-trunk— —
A mark more vertical, they tell me,
than the eyes of phantom branches.

For a while, I see only an aspen tree among its clones,
its narrow maze of dark marks on the pale
and no imitation emerging.
Must we train ourselves into the predator
and wait?

It happens to my eye—a touch of red,
a black diamond with short white stripes and spots.
Here, clinging like a magnet, it leans back on its tail,
placing its brush-like tongue to wells of sap
where small insects have stuck— —

Not all these musings are visible. Here, I say
passing the binoculars back. The trees flutter
their leaves like sequins under the deep
morning sky. The bird, still before me
or perhaps flown off, has vanished at this new distance.
Instead, these aspen congregate in a mass of wild grasses
between the hills and the dirt road
as if nothing were missing.

This Side of the Escarpment

The allure of the edge
lines the sky so it may
be the only line warning
bodies of the blue
there for falling.
Or is it an embrace
not yet reached,
bird with an askew wing
spiraling on?
I've attempted speech
with such nature
and found an echo,
found debris, grown
accustomed to empty
shells. Even those
found in the shoulder
of a mountain are shaped
as exoskeletons. Rarely
are they the body.
What I leave behind
I am ashamed
I cannot account for.
It's best the mealworm try to
transform it completely,
before it too hardens
a dark shell.

Tree Swallow / *Tachycineta bicolor*

Behind the window frame at dusk, swallows flock
in diagonal sweeps like ink so thick at times
they've disguised the horizon, and its gravity
is theirs pulling my body into a wave or a bird drawn,

and I will see myself from above—a point amid
or rather a point that could be me—for we are alike
when flying; I am here and also there and there,
and perhaps I am not the me or not what I thought:

I could be you. The you is an I as when one sees
themselves in a year before they were born,
but all along it was your mother in the photo.
You know it was her. But also 'me' from afar.

The collective us turns the world
on its head—the grass to sky, the mountains slumped
to the corners until the flow of us breaks
part to part. The birds and the bird in me disappear.

Neighborhood as Labyrinth

I begin with my hat, you with your keys.
Outside, the alleyway unfolds
lined with crowds of small, green apples.
The fence walks ahead
toward cut-away trees floating in chain-link,
toward vines, cinderblocks, telephone poles
until the faint shapes on the pavement—
collared doves and sparrows—disperse.
Looking back, we find no portrait.
The path's parallel lines threaten to meet
without us. Bare, overlapping trees embrace.
No one brought shadows under these gray skies.
We have reached our glen—
here is the bridge, here the water.
But return is not retracing.
My mother phones for seven minutes,
and just like that we're halfway back.
A and B were always neighboring points
of the same seed pattern,
so we race to catch the last and first steps.
Already, you've opened the door to let me in.

NOTES

"Dwellings and Decay" written after Chris Jordan's photo series of the Laysan albatross chicks on Midway Island. Without having developed the ability to regurgitate, many of these chicks die from consuming plastic waste.

"American Avocet / *Recurvirostra Americana*": According to The Cornell Lab of Ornithology, the American Avocet can make a defensive call that simulates the Doppler effect, making their approach seem faster than it is.

"Tomorrow" written after the "Go West" exhibit from the Buffalo Bill Center of the West that traveled to the University of Utah Museum of Fine Arts.

"This Side of the Escarpment": Mealworms, the larvae of the darkling beetle, can consume and digest the polystyrene. Recent studies show an interest in how this creature can help reduce plastic waste.

"Neighborhood as Labyrinth": A seed pattern is the beginning marks that provide the template for drawing a labyrinth. Oftentimes this means the entrance and center of the labyrinth are very close to one another.

ADDITIONAL ACKNOWLEDGMENTS

I am indebted to The Cornell Lab of Ornithology and The National Audubon Society databases, which fueled my research regarding certain species of birds I'd encountered.

Thank you to Katharine Coles, Paisley Rekdal, Jacqueline Osherow, and my University of Utah cohort for your aid in revising these poems.

Thank you to Nicole Walker for your insightful consultation. Your enthusiasm and direction was pivotal for me moving forward with this project.

And to Kitt Keller, thank you for your generous reading and thorough feedback. I'm so appreciative for your friendship. Thank you again Nicole and Jacqueline O. and also Adam Giannelli for your kind words on the completion of this project.

I am grateful for the love and support from my parents and my sisters. And to my husband, Chuy, I appreciate your listening ear, and I love the life we share.

Lastly, thank you to the natural spaces and species, which appear in these poems, for sharing with me your beauty and your dignity.

Jacqueline Balderrama grew up in Southern California and has a BA from UC Riverside and a MFA from Arizona State University. While at ASU, she received Virginia G. Piper Center Fellowships for international writing residencies in Asia and was involved in the Letras Latinas literary initiative and the ASU Prison Education Program.

Balderrama currently lives and teaches in Salt Lake City where she is a doctoral candidate in literature and creative writing at the University of Utah. Her poems received the 2013 Ina Coolbrith Memorial Poetry Prize, won a 2019 AWP Intro Journal Award, and have been published in *Blackbird*, *Poet Lore*, and other journals. She serves as co-poetry editor for *Quarterly West* and as poetry editor for *Iron City Magazine*.

Over the past six years, she has been working to reduce her waste and be mindful of the impacts human activity has on the planet. She shares a home with her husband and two small birds.

www.ingramcontent.com/pod-product-compliance
Lightning Source LLC
LaVergne TN
LVHW041505070426
835507LV00012B/1345